Are There Really Golden Cars on the Highways of Dubai?

Travel Book for Kids
Children's Travel Books

Speedy Publishing LLC
40 E. Main St. #1156
Newark, DE 19711
www.speedypublishing.com
Copyright 2017

All Rights reserved. No part of this book may be reproduced or used in any way or form or by any means whether electronic or mechanical, this means that you cannot record or photocopy any material ideas or tips that are provided in this book.

DUBAI is the biggest and most populous city in the United Arab Emirates (UAE) and is the capital of the Emirate of Dubai, which is one of the seven emirates that make up the UAE. In this book, we will be learning about this city, and we will find out if there really are gold cars on their highways!

WHERE IS DUBAI?

Dubai is located on the southeastern coast of the Persian Gulf. Dubai and Abu Dhabi are the only emirates that have power to veto critical matters of national importance in their country's legislature.

PERSIAN GULF MAP

Dubai has emerged to be a global city and a business hub for the Middle East. It also is a main transportation hub for cargo and passengers. Dubai's economy was based on its trade revenues by the 1960s, as well as, at a smaller extent, concessions for oil exploration; however, it was not until 1966 that oil was discovered. In 1969, the city's first revenue from oil began to flow.

This oil revenue has helped to accelerate the city's early development, but production levels are low and its reserves are limited. Less than five percent of the emirate's total revenue now comes from oil.

OIL FACTORY

Dubai's economy is driven by the western-style model of business, and its main revenues now come from aviation, real estate, tourism, and financial services. It was named recently by Salam Standard as the best destination for Muslim travelers. Dubai has recently been attracting world attention by several large innovative construction projects and sporting events.

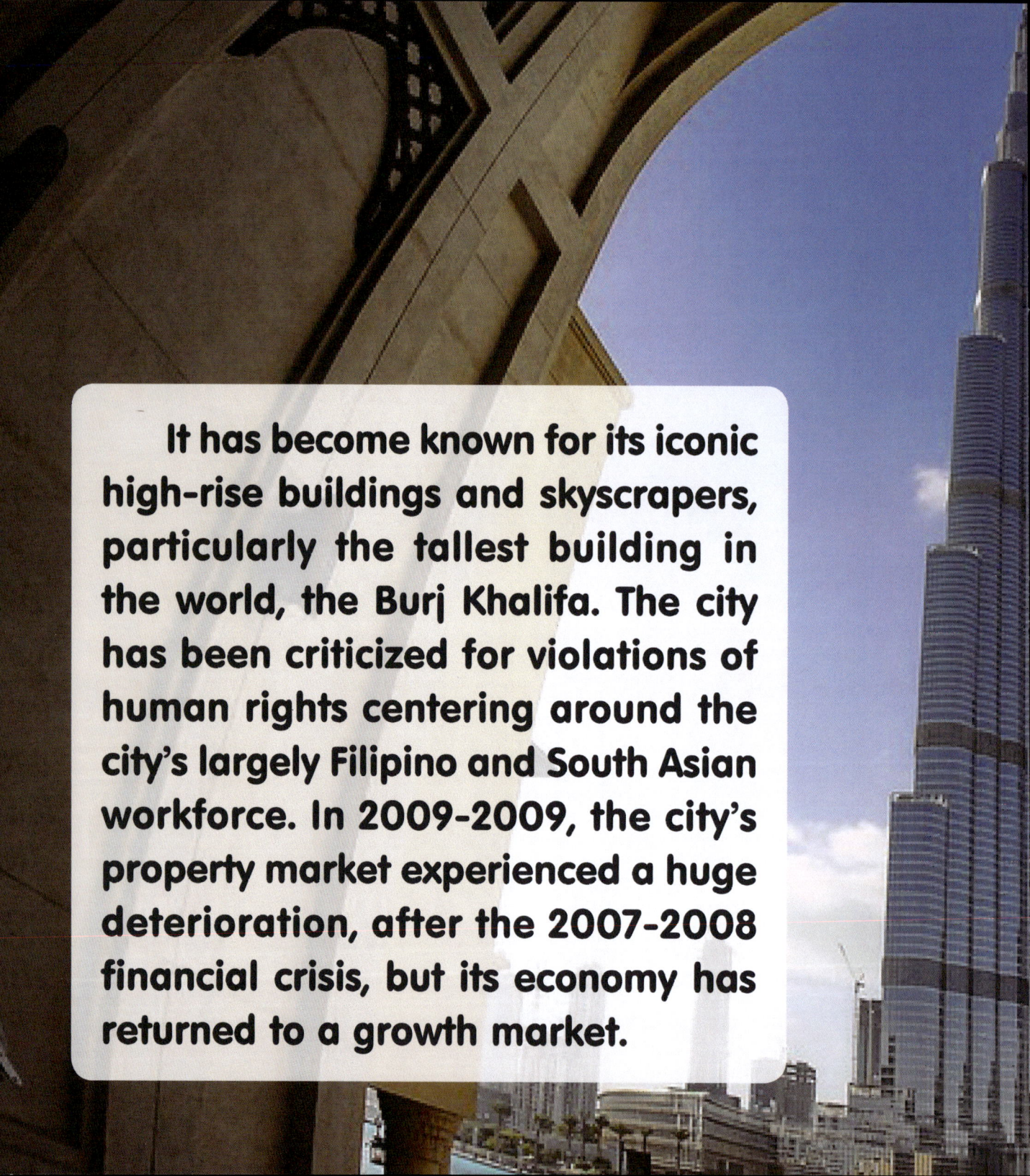

It has become known for its iconic high-rise buildings and skyscrapers, particularly the tallest building in the world, the Burj Khalifa. The city has been criticized for violations of human rights centering around the city's largely Filipino and South Asian workforce. In 2009-2009, the city's property market experienced a huge deterioration, after the 2007-2008 financial crisis, but its economy has returned to a growth market.

Dubai was rated as the 22nd most expensive city throughout the world as of 2012 and the Middle East's most expensive country. The hotel rooms in Dubai were the second most expensive throughout the world, following Geneva. It was rated to be one of the Middle East's best places to live.

There are more than 2 million people living in Dubai, but less than 15% of its population are made up of Emirati citizens (locals). Most are migrant workers from all over the world. Many are Asians, primarily from Bangladesh, India, Pakistan, as well as the Philippines, many brought in for temporary labor living in squalid conditions.

Making up around a tenth of the local population are Western nationals, many of them with tax-free, high-paying jobs, living the good life. There is an extreme class divide between these various groups.

TOURISM

An important part of this city's strategy is tourism which helps in maintaining flow of foreign cash into the emirate. Its lure for tourists is mainly based on its shopping, as well as its other ancient and modern attractions.

Dubai became the 7th most visited city throughout the world as of 2013, as well as being the fastest growing, at a rate of 10.7%. During 2016, it hosted 14.9 million overnight visitors, and is expected to increase to 20 million by 2020.

HOTEL IN DUBAI

Also known as the "shopping capital of the Middle East", Dubai has over 70 shopping centers, including the Dubai Mall, which is the largest shopping center in the world.

Dubai Creek Park also plays a key role in the city's tourism since it showcases many of the more famous attractions including the Cable Car, Dolphinarium, Horse Carriage, Exotic Bird Shows, and Camel Rides.

DOLPHINS AT DOLPHINARIUM

There are also many parks such as Mushrif park, Safa park, Hamriya park, and more. Each one is distinct from the other. Mushrif park shows unique houses throughout the world.

Ski Dubai consists of a big skiing facility indoor at the Mall of the Emirates, and offers ski lessons, snowboarding, a children's play area, as well as a café. It opened in November of 2005 and houses the largest indoor snow park throughout the world.

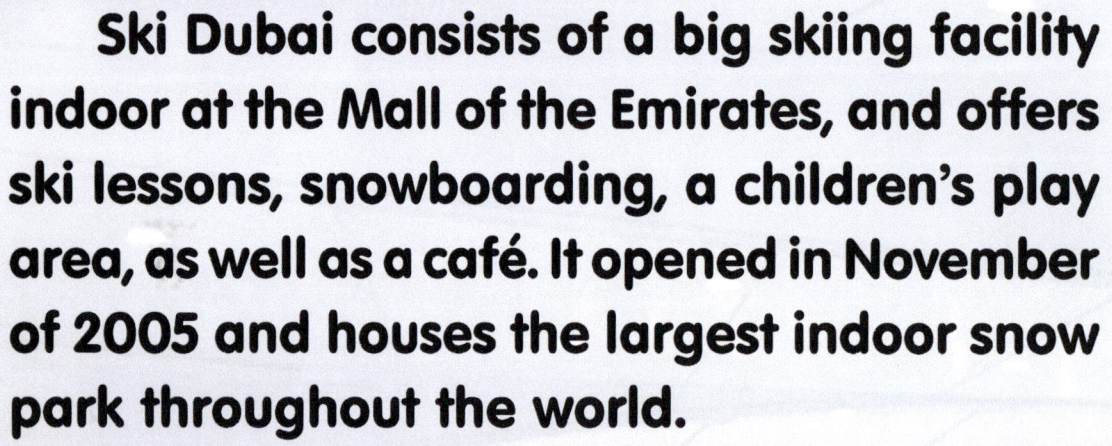

ARCHITECTURE

Dubai's skyline includes a rich collection of structures and buildings of varying styles of architecture. The world's tallest building can be found here, the Khalifa Tower (Burj Khalifa), at 2,722 feet (829.8 m). At the top, you will find the highest observatory deck in the world that has an outdoor terrace, which has become one of Dubai's more popular tourist attractions, having more than 1.87 million visitors during 2013.

THE BURJ AL ARAB HOTEL

This is a luxury hotel, often referred to as the only 7-star hotel in the world, even though the hotel's management has stated that it did not make such a claim.

The hotel's circular roof, typically used as a helipad for the rich and famous, can also be used as a sky-high tennis court. Roger Federer and Andre Agassi actually once played an exhibition match on this vertigo-inducing court.

BURJ KHALIFA

As discussed earlier, this is the tallest building in the world. Its inspiration came from the structure of the desert flower known as Hymenocallis. It was built with over 30 companies throughout the world and 100 nationalities of workers. It has become an icon of a building.

TRANSPORTATION

ROADS

Dubai transportation is governed by the Roads and Transport Authority, which is a government agency formed by a royal decree in 2005. In the past, the public transport network has faced reliability and congestion issues which has been addressed by a large investment program with a planned completion date of 2020. Also governed by the Roads and Transport Authority is the Public Bus Transport System as well as all taxi services.

AIR

Serving Dubai as well as other emirates in the country is Dubai International Airport, which is the hub for Emirates and Flydubai. In 2014, it was the seventh busiest airport in the world. It is also the seventh busiest cargo airport throughout the world.

AIRPLANE IN DUBAI AIRPORT

METRO RAIL

This $3.89 billion project consists of two lines (Green Line and Red Line) that run through the residential and financial areas throughout the city. This is the first urban train network throughout the Arabian Peninsula. All trains have automatic navigation and operate without a driver.

THE PALM JUMEIRAH MONORAIL

It opened on April 30, 2009 and is a monorail located on Palm Jumeirah. It runs from the Palm Jumeirah to the mainland.

CULTURE

The culture of UAE revolves mainly around the Islamic religion and Arab culture. This influence has been very prominent and can be seen in the city's music, architecture, cuisine, attire, and lifestyle. As a compromise between Friday's holiness for the Muslims and the Western weekend, their weekend consists of Friday through Saturday, rather than the Western weekend consisting of Saturday and Sunday.

The major holidays celebrated in Dubai include the end of Ramadan, known as Eid al Fitr, and National Day, celebrated on December 2, marking the formation of the UAE.

Muslim Celebrating Eid al Fitr

BURJ AL ARAB INTERIOR

THERE IS A REASON THEY CALL IT THE "CITY OF GOLD"

Dubai has more than 800 jewelry retailers. The luxury Burj Al Arab hotel's interior has a 24-carat gold leaf covering 1,790 square meters. Facial treatments using gold-leaf are offered by the Raffles Dubai Spa. Gold bars are even available for purchase in vending machines!

THE GOLD CARS

Yes, you will probably see gold cars traveling through the highways in Dubai.

Custom cars are seen as status symbols throughout the world, and Dubai is no exception. Approximately 2.2 million people live in Dubai, and around 26,000 are millionaires, or even billionaires.

GOLD CAR IN DUBAI

This means out of every hundred people that live there, one person in Dubai is sitting pretty with their wealth, and, basically being wealthy is no big deal. Consequently, the rich and the famous must get creative with their autos in order to one-up the next person.

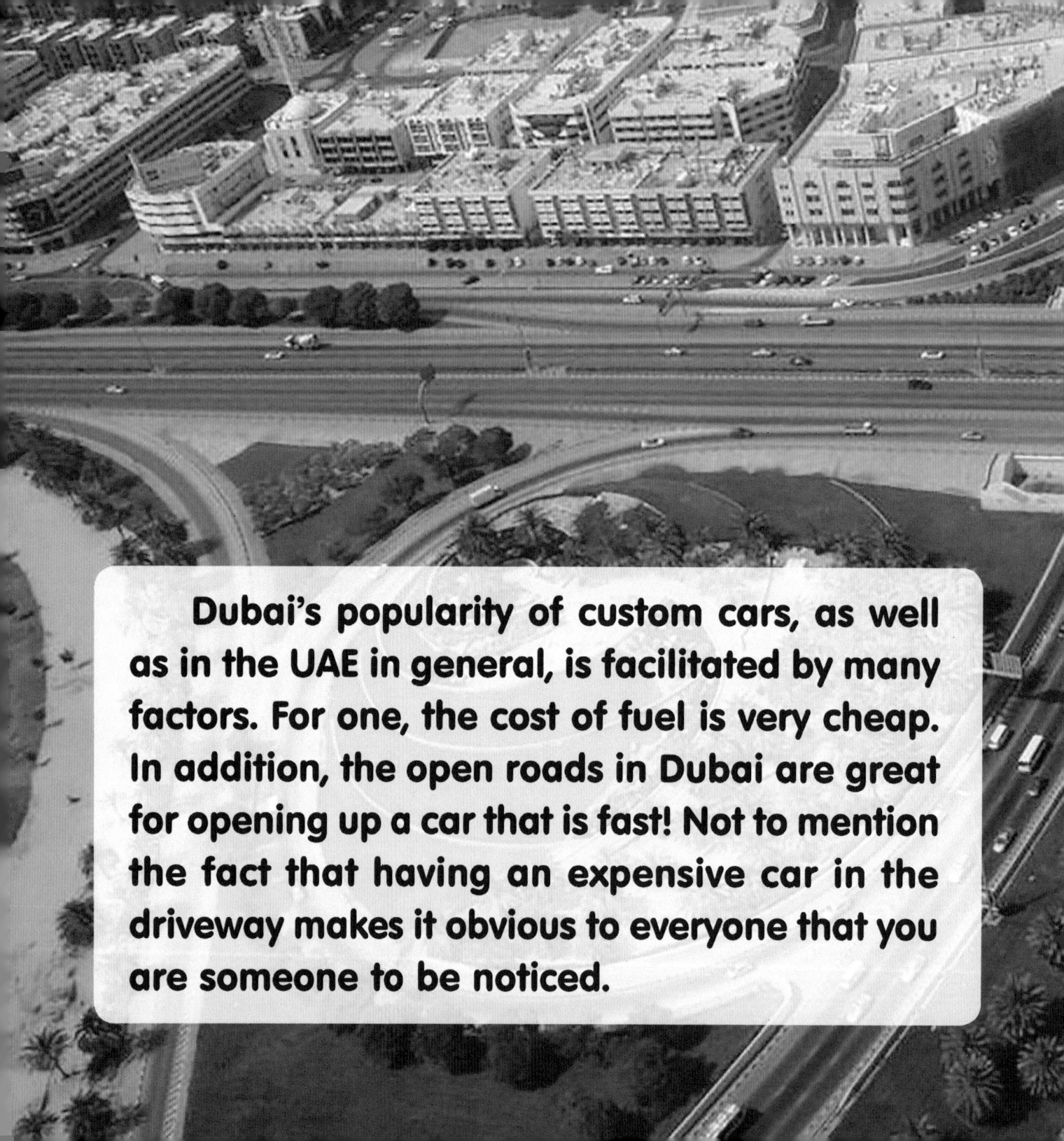

Dubai's popularity of custom cars, as well as in the UAE in general, is facilitated by many factors. For one, the cost of fuel is very cheap. In addition, the open roads in Dubai are great for opening up a car that is fast! Not to mention the fact that having an expensive car in the driveway makes it obvious to everyone that you are someone to be noticed.

GOLD MERCEDES

Among the gold cars are a gold decked sports utility vehicle, a gold Mercedes, and a gold Lamborghini. In addition to these cars, you might see a Mercedes coated with diamonds on show, but you will have to pay $1,000 just to touch it! And if you want to buy it, you will need $4.8 million! This is the world's most expensive car.

Dubai is full of amazing architecture and there is a lot to see and do in this beautiful city. To learn more about this city and the UAE, you can visit your local library, research the internet, and ask questions of your teachers, family and friends.

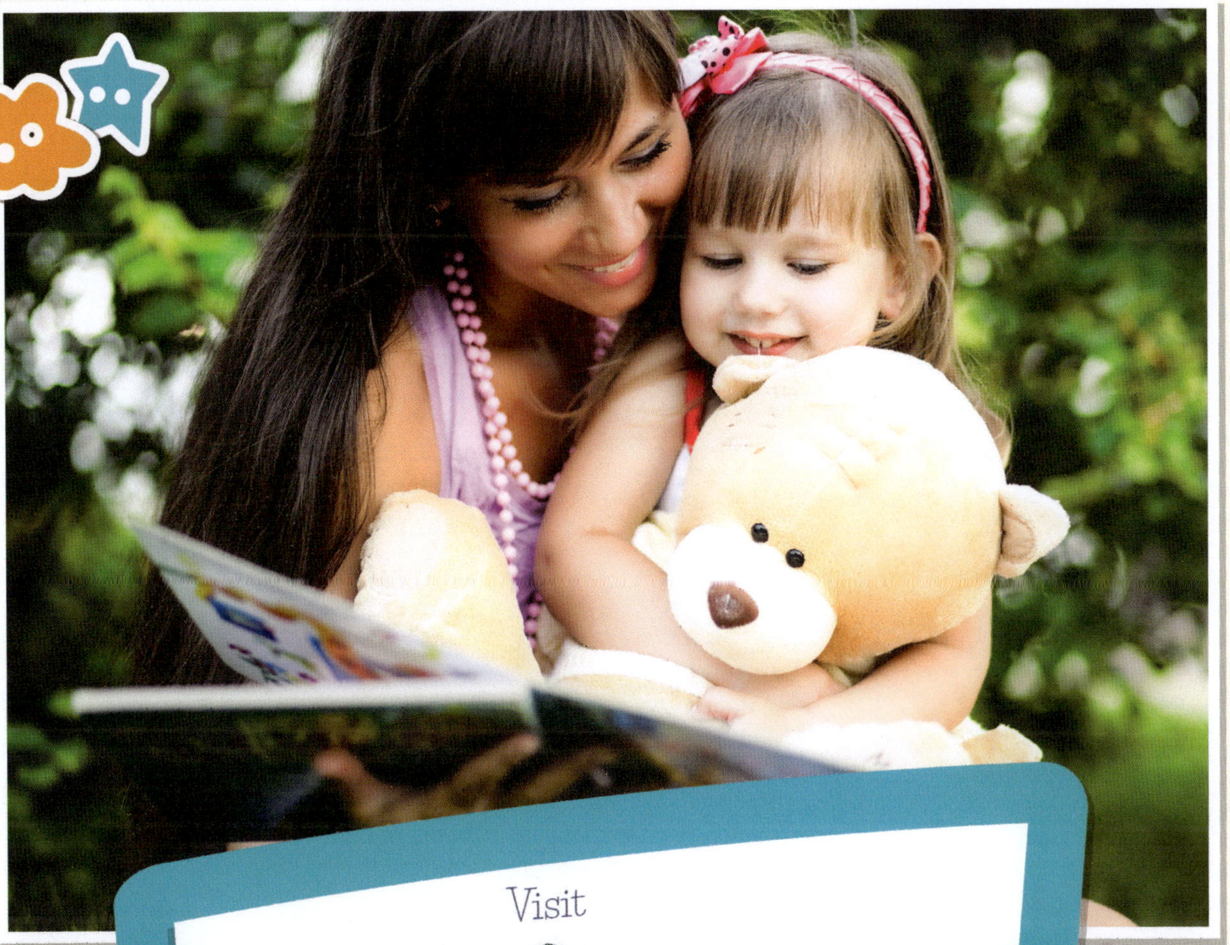

Visit

www.BabyProfessorBooks.com

to download Free Baby Professor eBooks
and view our catalog of new and exciting
Children's Books

Printed in Great Britain
by Amazon